MONEY, MONEY, MONEY

The Meaning of the Art and Symbols
on United States Paper Currency

NANCY WINSLOW PARKER

HarperCollinsPublishers

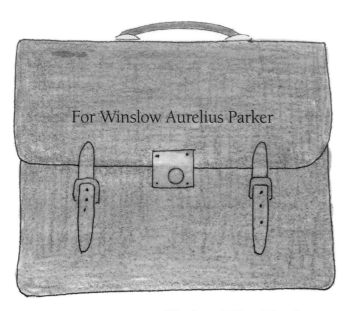

For Winslow Aurelius Parker

Woodrow Wilson's briefcase

Money, Money, Money
The Meaning of the Art and Symbols on United States Paper Currency
Copyright © 1995 by Nancy Winslow Parker
HarperCollins Children's Books, a division of HarperCollins Publishers,
10 East 53rd Street, New York, NY 10022.

Library of Congress Cataloging-in-Publication Data
Parker, Nancy Winslow.
   Money, money, money : the meaning of the art and symbols on United States paper currency / by Nancy Winslow Parker.
      p.   cm.
   ISBN 0-06-023411-3. — ISBN 0-06-023412-1 (lib. bdg.)
   1. Paper money—United States—History—Juvenile literature.   2. Signs and symbols—United States—History—Juvenile literature.   3. United States—History—Juvenile literature.
[1. Paper money—History.   2. Money—History.   3. Signs and symbols—History.]   I. Title.
HG610.P37   1995   93-43534
769.5'5973—dc20   CIP
                                                                 AC

1   2   3   4   5   6   7   8   9   10
❖
First Edition

Acknowledgments

Margaret Carmody, Federal Reserve Bank of New York, New York, New York; Beverly Rogers, Yale University Art Gallery, New Haven, Connecticut; Gene Hessler, St. Louis, Missouri; Bob Cochran, Society of Paper Money Collectors, Florissant, Missouri; Simon Schama, Mellon Professor of Social Studies, Harvard University, Cambridge, Massachusetts; Becky Simmons, Associate Librarian, George Eastman House, Rochester, New York; Richard H. Engeman, Photographs and Graphics Librarian, University of Washington Libraries, Seattle, Washington; Larry Viskochil, Curator of Prints and Photographs, Chicago Historical Society, Chicago, Illinois; Daniel J. Linke, Assistant Archivist, Seeley G. Mudd Manuscript Library, Princeton University, Princeton, New Jersey.

Washington, D.C.:
   L. W. Vosloh, National Numismatic Collection, Smithsonian Institution; Cecilia Wertheimer, Curator, Bureau of Engraving and Printing; Franklin Kelly, Curator of American Painting, National Gallery of Art; Catalina Vasquez Villalpando, 39th Treasurer of the United States, Department of the Treasury; Don A. Edwards, Assistant Director, Office of Government Liaison and Public Affairs, Department of the Treasury, U.S. Secret Service; Gerald T. Luchino, Institute of Heraldry, U.S. Army.

Peeking in Your Wallet

What is all that stuff on the $1 bill? Why are those tree leaves encircling the portrait on the $50 bill? Why is the government building in Washington, D.C., that appears on the $5 bill designed to look like an ancient Greek temple?

Paul Revere designed and engraved the first Continental paper money. Since then, bank notes and United States currency have been decorated with images of trains, Sioux Chief Running Antelope, bison, Martha Washington, Union General Philip Sheridan, Pilgrims, Pocahontas, and a 1914 battleship, to give a few examples.

In July 1929, after an eighteen-year study by the Treasury Department, the Bureau of Engraving and Printing began printing a redesigned, smaller-sized currency. The size of the bill was reduced from 7 7/16 by 3 1/8 inches to 6 5/16 by 2 11/16 inches so that twelve bills instead of eight would be engraved on one plate. The idea was copied from Philippine currency. The plan would save the government millions of dollars annually in production. Today the BEP prints thirty-two bills per plate.

A committee appointed by Secretary of the Treasury Andrew Mellon selected the portraits and vignettes that appear on the fronts and backs of today's bills. The committee wanted only presidential portraits, but Mellon insisted on three nonpresidents—Alexander Hamilton, Salmon P. Chase, and Benjamin Franklin. Committee notes reveal that they wanted Washington for the $1 bill because his portrait was familiar to everyone and because the $1 bill had the highest circulation. James Garfield was suggested for the $2 bill because he was a martyred president and his flowing beard would be a contrast to the clean-shaven Washington.

On the 1928 issue of Federal Reserve notes, and to this day, from the $1 bill to the $100,000 bill, you can find the history of the United States of America, from the days of the Founding Fathers and the early Republic to the World War I era when America emerged as a world power.

Our paper money has been called a lot of things—gelt, greenbacks, loot, jack, simoleons, rocks, scratch, spondulicks, wampum, sugar, bread, 10-spot, long green, smackers, the ready, moolah, shekels, wad, bucks, clams, dough, gravy, and sawbuck. It is, however, officially and soberly known today as Federal Reserve notes.

If you don't have one each of the $1, $2, $5, $10, $20, $50, $100, $500, $1000, $5000, $10,000, and $100,000 bills in your wallet, this book is the next best thing.

The Face of United States Currency

GEOMETRIC LATHE WORK—*A design made by a machine called a lathe that is impossible to copy (without the setting).*
ORNAMENT—*Embellishments around letters, numbers, and portraits.*

CHECK LETTER AND QUADRANT NUMBER—*Shows bill's position on printing plate of thirty-two bills.*
PORTRAIT—*All are former United States presidents except Alexander*

Hamilton, Benjamin Franklin, and Salmon P. Chase. No living person can be shown on United States currency or coin.
TREASURY SEAL—*Overprinted in green ink. Drives counterfeiters wild!*

SERIAL NUMBER—*Every bill has its own serial number. The first letter refers to the issuing Federal Reserve bank. The last letter refers to the print run (the first run is "A," the second is "B," etc.).*

FEDERAL RESERVE SEAL—*Identifies the Federal Reserve bank issuing this particular bill. Letters A through L match the first letter of the serial number.*

FEDERAL RESERVE NUMBER—*Appears four times on the bill.*
INSCRIBED SECURITY THREAD—*Wide polyester thread imbedded in paper, with printing on it*

to identify denomination of bill, such as "USA Twenty." Hold the bill up to the light to see.
MICROPRINTING—*Appears on the rim of the portrait to deter counterfeiters.*

SERIES IDENTIFICATION NUMBER—*Changes with each major design change and with a new secretary of the treasury. Letter at end of series date changes with a new treasurer or with a minor change in the bill.*

CHECK LETTER AND FACE-PLATE NUMBER—*Shows the plate that printed the bill. Letter is always the same as plate position letter in upper left corner.*

The Treasurer of the United States

The treasurer of the United States signs his or her name on the lower left side of all United States currency. The first treasurer of the United States was Michael Hillegas of Pennsylvania, who served from July 29, 1775, to September 11, 1789. Since then, there have been thirty-nine treasurers, and the past twelve have been women.

The treasurer of the United States is appointed by the president. The treasurer's duties include overseeing three Treasury bureaus, which are the Bureau of Engraving and Printing (BEP), the United States Mint, and the United States Savings Bond Division. The treasurer is also the chairperson for the Advanced Counterfeit Deterrence Steering Committee, which is comprised of members from the Federal Reserve System, the BEP, the Secret Service, and the Treasury Department. This committee advises the secretary of the treasury on measures to prevent counterfeiting of Federal Reserve notes. The treasurer's office is in the Treasury building on Pennsylvania Avenue in Washington, D.C.

Men treasurers *Women treasurers*

28   +   12   = 40

Michael Hillegas of Pennsylvania, first treasurer of the United States

40th treasurer of the United States (1993)

The Secretary of the Treasury

The secretary of the treasury's signature appears on the lower right face of all United States currency. The secretary is the head of the Treasury Department. This is one of the most important jobs in the United States government.

The secretary of the treasury is appointed by the president and approved by the Senate. The secretary is a member of the president's Cabinet, and he or she gives advice to the president on all matters related to money. Because of the importance of this Cabinet position it is second in rank after the secretary of state. The secretary of the treasury is part of the unofficial "inner Cabinet," which includes the secretary of state, the secretary of defense, and the attorney general.

There have been sixty-nine secretaries of the treasury, from Alexander Hamilton, appointed in 1789, to Lloyd Bentsen, appointed in 1992. The president usually appoints one or two secretaries during his term of office, but Andrew Jackson had five secretaries during his eight years in office, while James Madison had four secretaries.

Among the many duties of the secretary of the treasury are issuing checks; collecting taxes through the Internal Revenue Service; collecting customs duties; printing postage stamps, currency, and bonds; and chartering and inspecting banks. The secretary is also responsible for minting coins, a duty that dates back to 1792. The Treasury Department is in charge of the United States Secret Service, which protects the president and his family and tracks down counterfeiters of United States currency. There are 120,000 employees at the Treasury Department, up from five employees when the department was established in 1789.

Partial view of the president's Cabinet

Housing and Urban Development   Agriculture   Treasury   Gold bullion worth $140,000 per bar   Vice President   Attorney General

George Washington, 1732–1799

SURVEYOR, SOLDIER, FIRST PRESIDENT

George Washington was born in Virginia and grew up on a plantation. He planted crops, raised horses, worked with tools, and managed slaves. As a teenager, he worked as a surveyor, setting out new farms in the wilderness and exploring the frontiers. In the French and Indian Wars, he led Virginian colonial troops against the French in Ohio. The valuable experience he gained fighting with the British he later used against them as "General and Commander in chief of the army of the United Colonies and of all the forces raised for the defence of American Liberty." Washington was not a great thinker, but he was a great general and leader. After defeating the British, Washington resigned his commission and returned to his home at Mount Vernon, Virginia. In 1789, he was unanimously elected the first president of the United States and served two terms.

The engraving of Washington on the $1 bill is by George Frederick Cummings Smillie (1854–1924), after a painting by the American artist Gilbert Charles Stuart (1755–1828). Washington sat for the Atheneum head portrait in the spring of 1796 when he was sixty-four years old. He has powdered hair worn in a queue and tied with a bow, and he wears a black coat, white neckcloth, linen shirt ruffle, and lace jabot. Stuart painted three portraits of Washington from live sittings and then painted more than eighty copies of these paintings. The original Atheneum painting is owned jointly by the Museum of Fine Arts, Boston, and the National Portrait Gallery, Washington, D.C.

Laurel leaves

Laurel: ancient Greek symbol of victory

Sash of Commander in Chief

George Washington, Commander in Chief, Continental Army, 1777 (from a painting by Charles Willson Peale, 1779). Peale painted more than twenty-one copies of this painting.

Stars–ancient symbol of the spirit-light shining in the darkness

Glory of God

Out of many, one

American bald eagle

Congress

States

Arrows

Tail feathers

Shield

Olive branch

E Pluribus

Unum

Face

Eye of Providence

God has favored our undertakings

Pyramid of thirteen layers

Annuit

Coeptis

MDCCLXXVI

Novus Ordo Seclorum

New order of the ages

Reverse

The Great Seal of the United States

The Great Seal appears on important government papers, treaties, the cap of every enlisted man in the United States Army and Air Force, and on the $1 bill. The Great Seal was adopted by Congress on June 20, 1782.

On the face of the seal is the "Eagle of Democracy," representing American sovereignty. The head represents the executive branch, the shield the legislative branch (the blue bar symbolizes Congress and the thirteen red and white stripes symbolize the states), and the eagle's nine tail feathers represent the judicial branch. The eagle holds in his right talon an olive branch of thirteen leaves and thirteen olives, which represents peace, and in the left talon thirteen arrows, an American Indian war symbol,

which signifies the colonies' fight for liberty. Above the eagle's head is a "Glory of God," indicating the spiritual above the material.

The reverse shows an Egyptian pyramid representing "solid strength and duration." The "Eye of Providence" within a "Glory of God" indicates, again, the spiritual above the material. The unfinished pyramid means that the United States will build and grow in the future. The layers refer to the individual rights of the states, and the separate stones represent local self-government. The thirteen leaves, olives, arrows, layers, stars, letters in "E Pluribus Unum," and stripes represent the thirteen original colonies or states.

The original brass Great Seal is on public display in the National Archives, Washington, D.C. The Great Seal used today was engraved in hardened steel in 1904. It is on display in the Department of State, Washington, D.C.

Thomas Jefferson, 1743–1826

INVENTOR, ARCHITECT, THIRD PRESIDENT, STATESMAN

Thomas Jefferson, a philosopher of democracy, was one of the Founding Fathers. He grew up on a Virginia plantation where 150 slaves tended the tobacco and cotton crops. He was educated at the College of William and Mary, where he learned the classics, including writing in Greek. He held many important offices—minister to France, secretary of state, vice president, and president. Alexander Hamilton, who served in Washington's Cabinet with Jefferson, called him "a man of profound ambition and violent passions."

Carved on his simple tombstone are the three things he wanted to be remembered for—writing the Declaration of Independence (in seventeen days), writing the statute of Virginia for religious freedom, and being the father of the University of Virginia.

The 1867 engraving on the $2 bill is by Charles Burt, after an 1805 oil painting by Gilbert Charles Stuart. The painting is owned by Bowdoin College Museum of Fine Art, Brunswick, Maine. Stuart painted three copies: one was destroyed by fire in 1851; another, the Edgehill portrait, is jointly owned by the National Portrait Gallery and Monticello; and the third, painted 1810–1815, is hanging in the National Portrait Gallery of Art, Washington, D.C.

Thomas Jefferson as signer of the Declaration of Independence, 1776

9

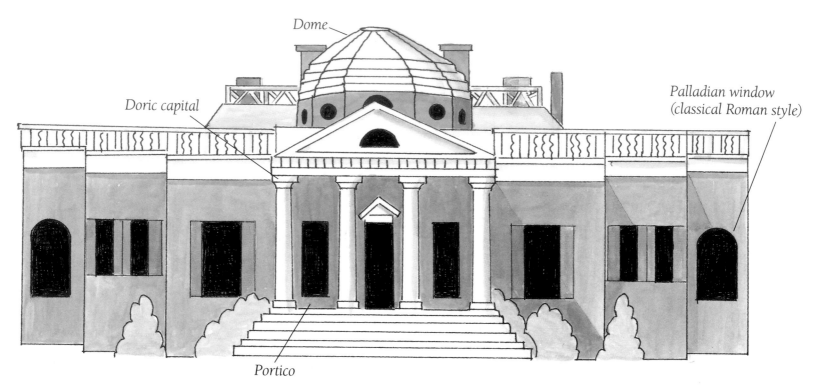

Dome

Doric capital

Palladian window
(classical Roman style)

Portico

Monticello

BEGUN 1770, REDESIGNED BETWEEN 1796 AND 1809

Monticello, the Charlottesville, Virginia, home of Thomas Jefferson, appears on the reverse side of the $2 bill issued in 1928. This vignette was dropped in 1976. Monticello is one of the most beautiful homes in America, designed by Jefferson in a simple yet elegant style after the architecture of ancient Greece and Rome. The building is made of brick, with white Doric columns on a portico. Monticello introduced a new style, inspired by Jefferson's classical studies, in American architecture.

This architectural landmark influenced future government buildings in Washington, D.C., which would be de-signed in early Republic or Federal style architecture, which was modeled on the classical Greek and Roman styles. Democracy, itself a product of Greek civilization and adopted by Jefferson and the Founding Fathers as the ideal form of government for the new America, would find a welcome home behind the familiar columns on the nation's capitol buildings.

Jefferson died at Monticello. Some of his inventions are still there, but his books were sold to the Library of Congress in 1815 to replace the ones burned by the British in the War of 1812. Monticello is situated on a hilltop, which is how it got its name—*monte cello*, Italian for "little mountain." The first floor is open to the public.

The 1928 engraving of Monticello is by Joachim C. Benzing.

John Trumbull
The Declaration of
Independence, 4 July 1776
*Yale University Art Gallery
Trumbull Collection*

*The five people standing in
front of John Hancock
(seated) are, left to right:
John Adams, Roger
Sherman, Robert Livingston,
Thomas Jefferson, and
Benjamin Franklin, the
drafters of the Declaration
of Independence.*

The Signing of the Declaration of Independence, 1776

In 1976, the Department of the Treasury issued a new reverse side for the $2 bill, and 225 million bills were printed to commemorate the 200th anniversary of the signing of the Declaration of Independence. The signing took place in the State House in Philadelphia, now Independence Hall.

The Declaration of Independence was adopted on July 4, 1776, and was signed on August 2, 1776, by fifty-six men from thirteen states. After signing, Benjamin Franklin said to John Hancock, "We must all hang together, or assuredly we shall all hang separately." On the $2 bill, three signers are dropped from each end of the vignette to allow the distinctive fibers in the paper to be seen.

The painting *The Declaration of Independence* is by John Trumbull (1756–1843), an American artist from Lebanon, Connecticut. He served briefly in the Continental Army and drew maps for General Washington. He knew most of the people he painted. The original (21⅛ by 31⅛ inches), painted 1786–1797, is located in the Trumbull Gallery, Yale University, New Haven, Connecticut. The painting in the rotunda of the United States Capitol is an enlarged version (12 by 18 feet) of the Yale original and was painted in 1818. A third version of *The Declaration of Independence* was painted in 1832 and hangs in the Wadsworth Atheneum in Hartford, Connecticut. Frederick Girsch engraved the painting in 1863.

The original Declaration of Independence is on exhibit in the National Archives building in Washington, D.C.

Abraham Lincoln, 1809–1865

SIXTEENTH PRESIDENT

Abraham Lincoln is known to all the world as the man who freed 4,000,000 slaves. After signing the Emancipation Proclamation, he said, "If my name ever goes into history, it will be for this act." He was president during the Civil War and spent his entire term of office in the company of armed guards. Lincoln himself never owned slaves, but nine other presidents did, including Washington, Jefferson, Jackson, Madison, and Grant.

During the Civil War, Lincoln was Commander in Chief of the Union forces even though he had scant knowledge of military affairs, having served only three months in 1832 in a volunteer militia during the Black Hawk War. He therefore wisely gave enormous authority to his generals, occasionally visiting battlefields but never meddling in the generals' decisions.

The portrait of Lincoln on the $5 bill was engraved by Charles Burt (1823–1892), an engraver at the Bureau of Engraving and Printing. His source was a photograph by Anthony Berger, who worked with the Brady Gallery. Berger was a partner of Mathew Brady, the "official" photographer of the Union Army in the Civil War. Lincoln sat for the portrait on February 9, 1864, in Washington. He is wearing a rich black broadcloth suit, white shirt, and black bow tie. Just one year later, Lincoln was shot by John Wilkes Booth at Ford's Theatre in Washington and died the next day, April 15, 1865. He is buried in Springfield, Illinois.

Confederate flag

Union flag

Abraham Lincoln, President and Commander in Chief, Civil War 1861–1865

Born: February 12, 1809, Hardin County, Kentucky

Forty-eight states
carved in attic

Attic

Doric capital

Thirty-six states
carved in frieze

Column

Portico

Stylobate

Terrace

Lincoln Memorial

BUILT 1911, COMPLETED 1922

The Lincoln Memorial was built during the Taft administration to honor Abraham Lincoln, an American hero second only to George Washington. It was designed by Henry Bacon (1866–1924), completed in 1922, and made of white Colorado-Yule marble. It sits in the middle of West Potomac Park, Washington, D.C.

The memorial is an excellent example of pure Greek temple design, very much like the ancient Parthenon in Athens. Thirty-six Doric columns, representing the thirty-six states in the Union at the time of Lincoln's death in 1865, circle around the exterior of the memorial. The names of the states are carved on the frieze. On the attic wall are carved the forty-eight states comprising the Union in 1922 and their dates of admission. Alaska and Hawaii, added in 1959, are inscribed in the terrace leading to the memorial. Within the memorial chamber is the large statue of the seated Lincoln, created by Daniel Chester French, the American sculptor (1850–1931). It is carved out of twenty-eight blocks of Georgia white marble and rests on a pedestal of Tennessee marble. Carved into the interior limestone walls are two plaques—one is Lincoln's Gettysburg Address, the other is his second inaugural address. In 1963, Martin Luther King Jr. gave his "I Have a Dream" speech from the steps of the Lincoln Memorial.

The 1927 engraving of the memorial on the $5 bill is by Joachim C. Benzing from an unknown source.

The Federalist
Article #1
signed: Publicus

Total number of
Federalist Papers: 85

Alexander Hamilton as
colonel, Continental Army,
1781

Alexander Hamilton, *1755–1804*

SOLDIER, STATESMAN,
FIRST SECRETARY OF THE TREASURY

Alexander Hamilton was born on the island of Nevis in the British West Indies and was educated at King's College (Columbia University). During the American Revolution, he was a dashing military hero in the Continental Army and fought in the battles of New York and New Jersey, finally becoming General Washington's aide-de-camp. At the Battle of Yorktown in 1781, Colonel Hamilton of Lafayette's light infantry led the assault on the left flank of General Charles Cornwallis' troops, contributing to the defeat of the British and their final surrender.

Hamilton, along with James Madison and John Jay, wrote the famous Federalist Papers (1787–88), a series of essays that appeared in New York newspapers and later were collected in a book, intended to explain the new federal government to the general public. When the new Cabinet was formed, Washington chose Hamilton as his secretary of the treasury.

In a dispute with political rival Aaron Burr, Alexander Hamilton was wounded in a duel and died the next day, July 12, 1804. He is buried in Trinity Churchyard, one block from the Federal Reserve Bank of New York in New York City.

The 1906 engraving of Alexander Hamilton is by George Frederick Cummings Smillie, after a painting by John Trumbull done in 1805, which hangs in City Hall, New York City.

The United States Treasury

BUILT 1836–1869

The first United States Treasury building was burned to the ground by the British in 1814. The second building was also destroyed by fire, in 1833. The present United States Treasury is the oldest of the government department buildings in Washington. It is located next to the White House on Pennsylvania Avenue. According to legend, Andrew Jackson, in an effort to end an argument over its site, thumped his walking stick on the ground and said, "Right here is where I want the cornerstone."

The five-story granite building was designed by Robert Mills (1781–1855) in the Greek Revival style. There are fifty-four granite Ionic and Corinthian columns around the exterior of the building. On the east facade alone there is a colonnade of thirty monolithic Ionic columns, each thirty-six feet high and all in an unbroken line of 341 feet!

Inside, fluted Corinthian columns flank broad marble corridors, and sweeping circular staircases go from floor to floor. Both the secretary of the treasury and the treasurer of the United States have their offices in this building. During the Civil War, the Treasury building served as a barracks for Federal troops.

The 1927 engraving of the Treasury building is by Louis S. Schofield from unknown sources.

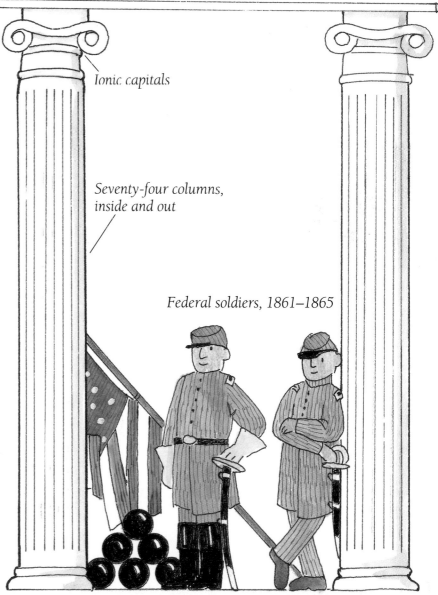

Monolithic Ionic column (made from a single large piece of stone)

Ionic capitals

Seventy-four columns, inside and out

Federal soldiers, 1861–1865

1928 automobile (a conglomerate of several models)

General Andrew Jackson, victor at the Battle of New Orleans, January 8, 1815

General Jackson's epaulette

Andrew Jackson, 1767–1845

SOLDIER, SEVENTH PRESIDENT

Andrew Jackson was born in a log cabin on the border of North Carolina and South Carolina. His military career began when he was a thirteen-year-old messenger for the Colonial troops in the American Revolution, and he rose to the rank of general in the War of 1812.

This war hero became our seventh president. However, Jackson was not everyone's hero. Thomas Jefferson said, "I feel much alarmed at the prospect of seeing General Jackson President. He is one of the most unfit men I know of for such a place." John Adams, the second president, thought he was a barbarian.

President Jackson fought the banks, engaged in one hundred duels, and fired his entire Cabinet. In 1838, he forced all the Cherokees living in Georgia, North Carolina, Tennessee, and Alabama to move to Indian Territory, now Oklahoma. This event is known today as the "Trail of Tears." By the 1840's, one fourth of the entire tribe was dead due to inhuman conditions on the trail.

The engraving of President Jackson on the $20 bill was done by Alfred Sealey in 1867, after a painting by American painter Thomas Sully (1783–1872). Sealey's engraving is from a study of a full-length portrait of Jackson in which he wears a black cloak with a velvet collar over a white ruffled shirt and black stock. The black uniform with brass buttons does not show in the engraving. The Sully painting is in the Detroit Institute of the Arts.

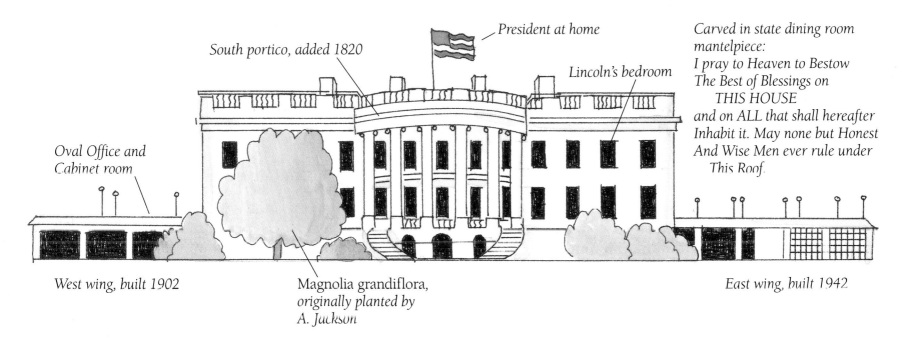

South portico, added 1820

President at home

Lincoln's bedroom

Carved in state dining room mantelpiece:
*I pray to Heaven to Bestow
The Best of Blessings on
THIS HOUSE
and on ALL that shall hereafter
Inhabit it. May none but Honest
And Wise Men ever rule under
This Roof.*

Oval Office and Cabinet room

West wing, built 1902

Magnolia grandiflora, originally planted by A. Jackson

East wing, built 1942

The White House

BUILT 1792, REBUILT 1817, RESTORED 1948–1950

The White House, located at 1600 Pennsylvania Avenue in Washington, D.C., is the official residence of the president of the United States. It is also the symbol of American power and position in the world. It was designed by Philadelphia architect James Hoban in the Palladian style, based on some eighteenth-century houses in Dublin, Ireland. The cornerstone was laid in 1792 and tapped into place by Collen Williamson, the master mason.

The exterior of the White House is constructed of white-grey Virginia sandstone and painted white to seal the porous rock. It was burned by the British in 1814 and rebuilt in 1817. The north and south porticos, designed by Benjamin Henry Latrobe, were added in the 1820's.

Porticos are features of ancient Roman villas intended for open-air living.

The interior of the White House has 132 rooms, some as big and sumptuous as those in the palace of a king. Thomas Jefferson said the White House was "big enough for two emperors, one pope, and the grand lama."

The White House is also the president's office. The west wing was added to accommodate the Executive Department offices and staff. The east wing is built on ground once occupied by greenhouses and consists of a visitors' entrance, a garden reception room, and a glass-enclosed colonnade leading to the White House.

During Harry S. Truman's administration, the White House was completely restored. The engraving of the White House showing the new second-floor balcony, two additional chimneys, and larger trees and shrubbery was done by Charles A. Brooks in 1948.

Ulysses S. Grant, 1822–1885

SOLDIER, EIGHTEENTH PRESIDENT

Oak leaves—ancient Roman symbol of strength and long life

General Grant's shoulder board

Although Ulysses S. Grant appears on the $50 bill as the eighteenth president of the United States, he was chosen not because of his administration, one of the most corrupt and scandal-ridden in United States history, but because of his military career and his inspired leadership during the Civil War.

Grant graduated from the United States Military Academy at West Point, served in the Mexican War and for a short time in Pacific Northwest forts, but retired shortly thereafter. He was drawn back into the service at the outbreak of the Civil War and rose to be "General in Chief of the Union Forces," the first soldier to attain that rank since George Washington. He accepted the surrender of Confederate General Robert E. Lee at Appomattox Court House on April 9, 1865, thus ending the Civil War.

Grant died penniless. He is buried in Grant's Tomb, a magnificent mausoleum in New York City. At the dedication in 1897 by President William McKinley, his grateful country staged one of the greatest parades ever seen in the United States.

The engraving of General Grant on the $50 bill was done by John Eissler in 1927 from a photograph by an unknown photographer taken around 1876.

Ulysses S. Grant, General U.S.A., Civil War, 1861–1865

West Point Cadet 1839–1843

Mexican War 1845

President 1868–1876

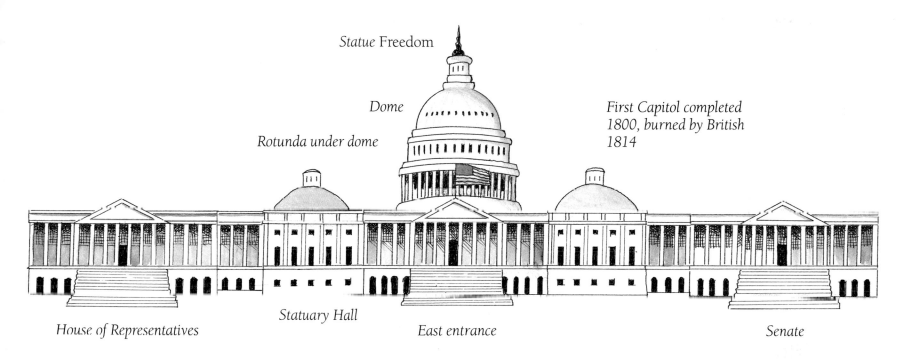

Statue Freedom

Dome

First Capitol completed
1800, burned by British
1814

Rotunda under dome

Statuary Hall

House of Representatives

East entrance

Senate

The Capitol

The United States Capitol is the symbol of our government. It is located on Capitol Hill, formerly called Jenkins Hill and the site of an old Indian village, and it dominates Washington, D.C. It was designed by William Thornton, a West Indian doctor who had no architectural training. George Washington laid the cornerstone in 1793.

The building is mostly a Classical Roman style of architecture with some Greek and Renaissance details. The 287-foot-5½-inch-tall cast-iron dome, painted to look like marble, is based on Michelangelo's plan for the dome of St. Peter's Church in Rome. The interior circular temple, or rotunda, is wonderfully spacious, with light coming in

through windows in the crown of the dome. As late as 1958 the Capitol underwent expansion, in this case a 32½-foot extension of the east front.

The most popular aspect of the United States Capitol is by far the interior corncob and tobacco leaf capitals designed by Benjamin Henry Latrobe. They received "more applause from members of Congress . . . than all the Works of Magnitude that surround them." At the very top of the dome is the 19½-foot, 15,000-pound bronze statue *Freedom*, a formless, bulky female by American sculptor Thomas Crawford (1814–1857). The 1927 engraving of the Capitol is by Louis S. Schofield.

Benjamin Franklin, *1706–1790*

PRINTER, INVENTOR, POSTMASTER, STATESMAN

Benjamin Franklin was born in Boston, the fifteenth of seventeen children. The multitalented Franklin considered himself foremost a printer. He printed money for the government, bank bills for New Jersey, and the highly successful *Poor Richard's Almanac*. In one issue he wrote, "In rivers and in bad governments, the lightest things swim at the top."

Franklin held many important positions, including member of the second Continental Congress, minister to England, minister to France, and delegate to the Constitutional Convention. Franklin was to become the only American to have signed all four key American documents: the Declaration of Independence in 1776, the Treaty of Alliance with France in 1778, the Treaty of Paris I in 1783 (the peace treaty with Great Britain that ended the American Revolution), and the Constitution in 1787. Franklin died in 1790 and is buried in the graveyard of Christ Church, Philadelphia.

The $100 bill is the highest denomination of currency circulated among the general public. The portrait of Franklin on this bill was engraved by John Eissler in 1928, based on an engraving by R. W. Dodson of an oil painting by J. B. Longacre. The painting shows Franklin with long white hair and wearing a red coat with a brown fur collar, white stock, and ruffled shirt. Longacre copied *his* painting from one attributed to J. S. Duplessis, painted in 1778 in Paris. The Longacre/Duplessis portrait hangs in the Governor's Office, Harrisburg, Pennsylvania.

Benjamin Franklin, printer

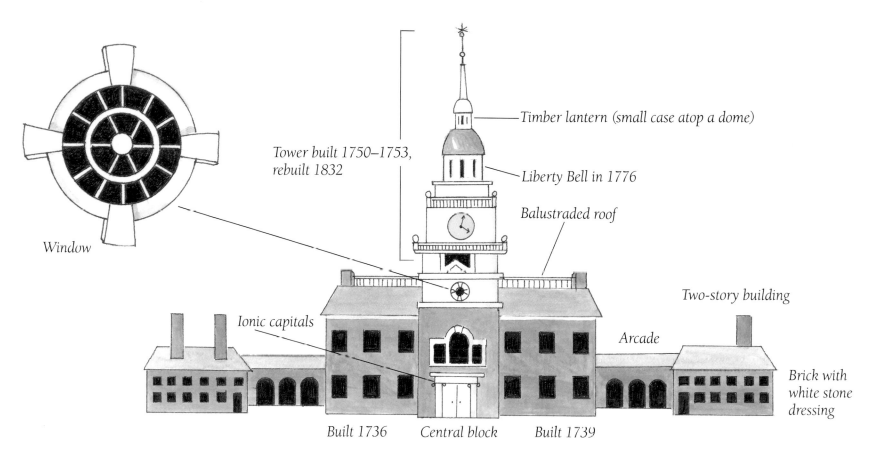

Window

Tower built 1750–1753, rebuilt 1832

Timber lantern (small case atop a dome)

Liberty Bell in 1776

Balustraded roof

Two-story building

Ionic capitals

Arcade

Brick with white stone dressing

Built 1736   Central block   Built 1739

Independence Hall

BUILT 1731–1791

Independence Hall, the former State House, Philadelphia, is the symbol of the nation's beginnings—the place where the patriots met and signed the Declaration of Independence in 1776.

The building is designed in the English Georgian style, which was the popular architectural style in the eighteenth century. The colonial Quakers of Philadelphia wanted their public buildings to look like their homes back in England but on a larger scale, to proclaim their official function. Independence Hall has the finest Georgian tower on either side of the Atlantic.

The Liberty Bell, cast by Thomas Lister in Whitechapel, London, was installed in the tower in 1752. It cracked and was recast. In 1776, the bell announced the first public reading of the Declaration of Independence to Philadelphians. The bell weighs 2,080 pounds, has a clapper 3 feet 2 inches long, and is currently on exhibit in Independence National Historical Park, Philadelphia.

Millions of visitors come to Independence Hall every year. However, the 264-year-old building is deteriorating and is in grave danger of burning to the ground. The National Park Service has planned extensive renovation.

The 1928 engraving of Independence Hall on the $100 bill is by Joachim C. Benzing from unknown sources.

Lieutenant's insignia,
U.S.A., Civil War

William McKinley, second
lieutenant, 23rd Ohio
Volunteer Infantry, U.S.A.,
Civil War

William McKinley, 1843–1901

SOLDIER, STATESMAN, TWENTY-FIFTH PRESIDENT

William McKinley, the son of an iron manufacturer, was born in Niles, Ohio, the seventh of nine children. He attended Allegheny College and at the outbreak of the Civil War enlisted in the 23rd Ohio Volunteer Infantry. At the Battle of Antietam, he carried food and water to the troops under heavy fire, and he was present at the Battle of Cedar Creek, witnessing General Philip Sheridan's famous ride. At the end of the war he was a major.

Although stiff, cold, and rigid, McKinley was endowed with reason, common sense, and legendary courtesy. He was elected to the House of Representatives, and he was the governor of Ohio and the twenty-fifth president.

During his administration, the battleship USS *Maine* was blown up in Havana Harbor, and 260 sailors were killed, thus starting the Spanish-American War. In a gesture to the South, which had been defeated just thirty-three years earlier in the Civil War, McKinley commissioned Joseph Wheeler, a former Confederate general, to be a major general of volunteers in the Spanish-American War. American troops invaded Cuba and defeated the Spanish, who ceded the Philippines, Guam, and Puerto Rico to the United States. While on a visit to Buffalo, New York, McKinley was shot by an assassin and died eight days later, on September 14, 1901.

The 1928 engraving of McKinley on the $500 bill is by John Eissler. His source was a photo by Rockwood Studios, New York, circa 1896.

Grover Cleveland, *1837–1908*

TWENTY-SECOND AND TWENTY-FOURTH PRESIDENT

Although Grover Cleveland was the first president to be married in the White House, that is not the reason his portrait appears on the $1,000 bill. It is because he was a major political figure and a great American.

Cleveland was born in Caldwell, New Jersey, the son of a Presbyterian minister. He had been a lawyer, sheriff, mayor, and governor of the state of New York. He rose to the highest office in the land by being honest and using his common sense. At his first inaugural address, Cleveland said of democracy, " . . . the laws and the entire scheme of our civil rule, from the town meeting to the State capitals and the national capital, [are] yours."

During Cleveland's presidencies, United States currency was based on the gold standard, which meant that currency could be changed into gold at any time. United States gold was held in reserve in the form of gold bars, or bullion. Cleveland's administration was beset with a financial panic, a railroad strike, high tariffs, and unemployment, all of which he solved with wise but unpopular decisions. He added one person to the Cabinet—the secretary of agriculture. Time has proven Cleveland one of the ablest presidents of the modern era.

The 1927 engraving of Cleveland is by John Eissler from an unknown source.

President Grover Cleveland and Mrs. Cleveland, the former Frances Folsom, at their White House wedding

$5000

James Madison, 5'6" tall, 100 pounds, blue eyes, powdered hair—circa 1822, after Gilbert Charles Stuart

Bill from the 1918 series

White stock, ruffled shirt

Dolley Madison, wife of James Madison, saves state papers from the burning White House.

British burn White House in War of 1812.

James Madison, 1751–1836

STATESMAN, FOURTH PRESIDENT

James Madison, known as "The father of the United States Constitution," was born in Virginia, educated at Princeton, and became a member of the Continental Congress. He helped frame the Bill of Rights and wrote the Federalist Papers with Alexander Hamilton and John Jay. James Madison wrote in one of the Federalist Papers (XIII, 1788), "In a Democracy, the people meet and exercise their government in person; in a Republic, they administer it by their representatives and agents. A Democracy, consequently, will be confined to a small spot. A Republic may be extended over a large region."

After his presidency, James Madison made his home at the beautiful Montpelier estate near Culpepper, Virginia, where he lived life to the hilt, finally dying at the brink of insolvency. The estate is now run by the National Trust for Historic Preservation.

The portrait of Madison on the $5,000 bill was engraved by Alfred Sealey in 1869, after an oil painting by Gilbert Charles Stuart. Stuart painted several portraits of Madison. The one at Amherst College in Amherst, Massachusetts, painted in 1822, is most likely the source for the engraving. Other portraits of Madison by Stuart are owned by Colonial Williamsburg, Bowdoin College Museum of Fine Art, and the National Portrait Gallery. Another was destroyed by fire in 1851.

Salmon P. Chase, *1808–1873*

TWENTY-FIFTH SECRETARY OF THE TREASURY

Salmon Portland Chase, the eighth of eleven children, was born in New Hampshire and raised by his uncle, Philander Chase, the Episcopal Bishop of Ohio. During his lifetime, Chase held many important offices, such as secretary of the treasury in Abraham Lincoln's administration. His major achievement as secretary was saving the Union by his brilliant financing of the Union's military effort in the Civil War.

In 1864, Chase ordered "In God We Trust" to appear on all coins minted during the Civil War. Almost one hundred years later, Congress ordered "In God We Trust" to appear on all United States currency.

Salmon Chase was ambitious but difficult. He threatened to resign four times while he was secretary of the treasury, and he conducted an anti-Lincoln movement while still in Lincoln's Cabinet, calling the meetings "useless" and distrusting Lincoln's manner of carrying out public business. Lincoln eventually accepted Chase's resignation, having run out of patience with his disruptive Cabinet officer. Chase really wanted to be president and tried several times to be nominated by his party, but he lost each time. Lincoln finally stabilized this "loose cannon" by appointing him Chief Justice of the Supreme Court. Chase presided over the impeachment of President Andrew Johnson in 1868 with notable fairness.

The Chase portrait on the $10,000 bill is by an unknown American Bank Note engraver, circa 1861, from an unknown source.

Completely outfitted soldier, U.S.A., Civil War, 1861–1865

Salmon P. Chase, twenty-fifth secretary of the treasury

Woodrow Wilson, 1856–1924

EDUCATOR, TWENTY-EIGHTH PRESIDENT

Woodrow Wilson, like Grover Cleveland, was the son of a Presbyterian minister. He studied at various schools, and after twenty-five years in the field of education, he became president of Princeton University. He was elected governor of the state of New Jersey, and at the Democratic presidential convention he was nominated on the forty-sixth ballot.

Wilson is considered a great American and worthy of being represented on United States currency. During his first administration, Wilson sent troops to occupy Veracruz, Mexico, to protect American interests. Wilson mediated the delicate situation and avoided a declaration of war. During his second administration, Wilson, a president with no military training, declared war on Germany. The United States entered World War I and sent troops to Europe for the first time. In 1918 Wilson broke a presidential tradition by heading the United States peace delegation to Paris. He was awarded the Nobel Peace Prize. After the war, the idealistic Wilson founded the League of Nations, only to have Congress refuse to allow the country to join it. His ideals would reappear years later in the creation of the United Nations.

The Bureau of Engraving and Printing issued 42,000 copies of the $100,000 bill with Wilson's portrait. They were never intended for general circulation but are used in transactions between Federal Reserve banks. The portrait was engraved by George Frederick Cummings Smillie in 1913 from a photo by the Moffett Studio, Chicago, circa 1912.

Woodrow Wilson, President, Princeton University

Ph.D. gold tassel

Ph.D. blue

"The use of a University is to make young gentlemen as unlike their fathers as possible."
Woodrow Wilson
October 24, 1914
Pittsburgh,
Pennsylvania

Engraving and Printing

The Bureau of Engraving and Printing (BEP) began in 1862 with six people working in the basement of the main Treasury building. Today, the Bureau of Engraving and Printing is located at 14th and C Streets SW, one block south of the Washington Monument. Tall Doric columns surround the exterior of the building. Within the building, the government designs and prints United States currency, from the $1 bill to the $100 bill. The BEP stopped printing the $500 bill and all other bills above that denomination in 1969 because there was little demand and it is much safer to write checks or use credit cards. The large denominations are used only in bank business between the Federal Reserve and the Treasury Department. The BEP also prints postage stamps.

In this vast building, engravers work for months on a steel engraving of a portrait, vignette, ornament, or lettering, which will appear on today's currency. On a tour of the building, visitors can see the high-speed sheet-fed rotary presses printing 8,000 sheets of money per hour, and see the final stacks of shrink-wrapped notes ready to be shipped to the twelve Federal Reserve districts throughout the United States.

In 1991, BEP established a plant in Fort Worth, Texas, to print $1 and $5 bills. On Fort Worth notes, the letters "FW" precede the check letter and face-plate number. Sometimes mistakes happen. The BEP destroys imperfect notes and replaces them with "star" notes that have an asterisk on them after the serial number in place of the suffix letter (e.g., B65341959*). An asterisk is also used for the 100,000,000th bill in a series.

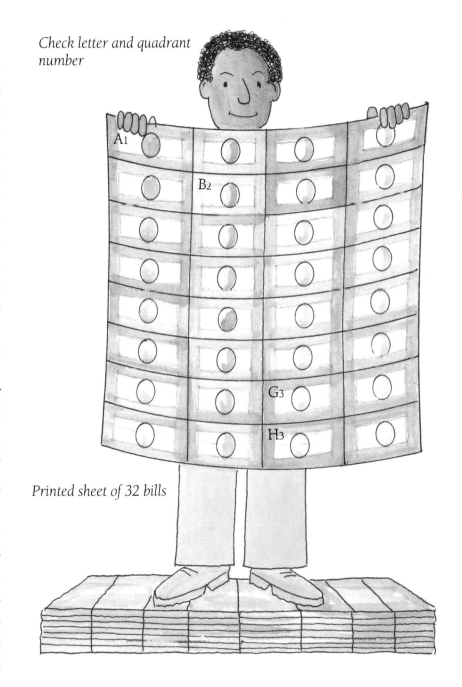

Check letter and quadrant number

Printed sheet of 32 bills

Counterfeiters

Counterfeiting is one of the oldest crimes in the world. It means defrauding, falsely making, forging, or altering any form of security of government, such as currency, coins, bonds, and checks. One grand form of counterfeiting occurs when one country counterfeits another country's currency in order to destabilize its economy, thus waging a form of war. During the American Revolution, the British counterfeited so much Continental currency that it became practically worthless.

The first paper money actually issued by the federal government was to finance the Civil War. Because the bills were printed with green ink on the back, they were nicknamed "greenbacks." During the Civil War, between one third and one half of all currency in circulation was counterfeit. It was a major achievement of Lincoln's Secretary of the Treasury Salmon P. Chase that the currency situation was rectified. Most paper currency circulating between the Civil War and World War I consisted of bank bills printed by a multitude of state-chartered private banks. The bills had a wide variety of portraits, vignettes, designs, and ornaments that came in all sizes and colors. The resulting confusion allowed counterfeiters to easily produce fake bills that began to appear everywhere.

Hugh McCulloch, Lincoln's third secretary of the treasury, established the United States Secret Service in 1865 to combat the counterfeiting of United States currency. William P. Wood, veteran of the Mexican War and keeper of the Old Capitol Prison, was appointed chief of the new Secret Service division. He sent his "operatives" out into the field, and in one year, the Secret Service had captured more than two hundred counterfeiters and destroyed many counterfeiting plants.

Today, there are millions of counterfeit bills in the world, and the United States is a prime target of counterfeiters. Counterfeiters are not ordinary felons. They are usually intelligent, semiskilled artisans who think they can get away with fooling the government. In jail, they are admired by other inmates. In the past, a counterfeiter was a lone engraver counterfeiting bills by hand, whereas today's counterfeiter may be a printer with a high-speed press, dedicated to outwitting the federal agents. In fact, photographers in printing plants often shoot a copy of a United States bill just to see what it looks like—and there are thousands of printing plants in the United States!

Advances in computer, copier, laser, and printing technology provide a counterfeiter with more opportunities to try his or her hand, but the crime is a risky one. The Secret Service says it suppresses approximately 90 percent of counterfeit currency before it reaches the public. It has on file a copy of almost every single counterfeit bill made since 1929. Counterfeiters are sent to jail, either federal or state prison. The maximum sentence is fifteen years.

There are many measures taken today by the Treasury Department to thwart the counterfeiting of United States currency. Some of them are as follows:

PORTRAITS—Engravers at BEP specialize in picture engraving (portraits, vignettes, and ornament) or in letter engraving (letters, numbers, and script). Picture engravers serve a ten-year apprenticeship and letter engravers serve a seven-year apprenticeship.

A genuine portrait on United States currency appears lifelike and has fine lines in the background. Counterfeit portraits are flat, and the background is dark and mottled.

BORDERS—The beautiful, complex border designs on a bill are produced by a geometric lathe. The fine lines in the outer margin and scrollwork are nearly impossible to counterfeit. If it is attempted, the result is blurred and indistinct when photographed.

SEAL—The Treasury seal, overprinted in green on every bill, has clear, distinct, sawtooth points. Counterfeit seals may have uneven, blunt, or broken points.

PAPER—The red and blue fibers embedded in the paper are unavailable to counterfeiters, as is the off-white-colored paper. Paper content is twenty-five percent linen, seventy-five percent cotton. Counterfeiters try to simulate these fibers by printing tiny red and blue lines on their paper. But these are printed on the surface, not embedded in the paper. It is against the law to try to manufacture the paper used in United States currency.

SECURITY THREADS—Inscribed security threads (e.g., "USA TWENTY" is repeated across the width of the bill) made of polyester are embedded in bills of series 1990. Currently present in $10 denominations and higher.

MICROPRINTING—Microprinting appears on the rim of the portrait on $10 denominations and higher, beginning with series 1990. The words "THE UNITED STATES OF AMERICA" are repeated around the portrait. Eventually, all denominations,

except the $1 bill, will have microprinting.

SECRETS—Secret formulas are used in the manufacture of the paper and the inks.

One of America's most famous counterfeiters, M. M. Landress, was able to pass almost perfect counterfeit currency until he was caught. But he never went to jail or paid a fine. Instead, he went to work for the United States government, helping to catch other counterfeiters and to develop anticounterfeiting devices. Mr. Landress said, "The basic look of our money . . . [is] an elegant, uncluttered look that makes it to my eyes the best d__ money in the world."

Because of the rise in the counterfeiting of U.S. currency, the Treasury Department in 1994 announced that it will make big changes in the design of the currency. The changes will take time, so it will be years before the newly designed currency is in the hands of the public.

WANTED

M. CHGO. P.D.
CB 3880931

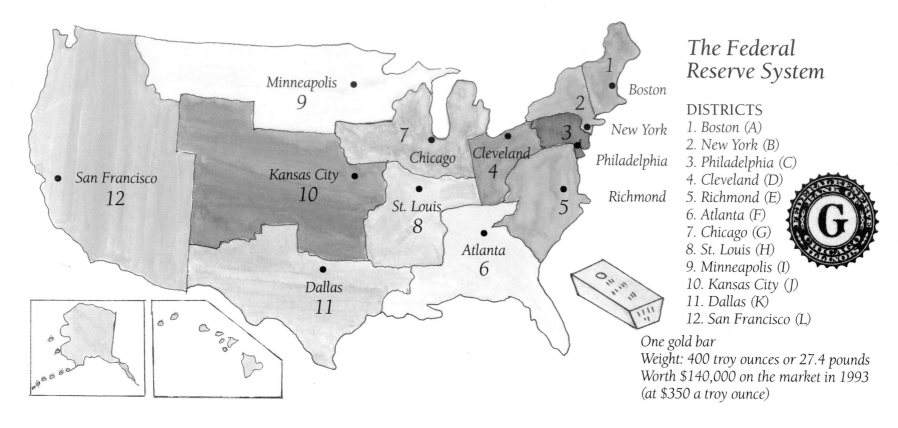

The Federal Reserve System

DISTRICTS
1. Boston (A)
2. New York (B)
3. Philadelphia (C)
4. Cleveland (D)
5. Richmond (E)
6. Atlanta (F)
7. Chicago (G)
8. St. Louis (H)
9. Minneapolis (I)
10. Kansas City (J)
11. Dallas (K)
12. San Francisco (L)

One gold bar
Weight: 400 troy ounces or 27.4 pounds
Worth $140,000 on the market in 1993
(at $350 a troy ounce)

The Federal Reserve

The Federal Reserve System was established by the Federal Reserve Act of 1913. As the central bank of the United States, the Federal Reserve System has many functions, including conducting monetary policy and regulating banks. There are twelve Federal Reserve banks in the United States, located in major cities of the Federal Reserve districts. Their seal is on the face of all United States currency. They receive their printed currency directly from the Bureau of Engraving and Printing. The Federal Reserve bank and its branches separate out the damaged and soiled currency from their viable currency. They count the damaged currency, shred it, and then compact it into briquettes. These briquettes are generally thrown away, but sometimes they are used as roofing shingles or as insulation!

The Federal Reserve Bank of New York on Liberty Street holds 312 million troy ounces of gold bullion, belonging to various foreign central banks, in its sub-basement vault. In 1993, the value of the gold was $109.2 billion (at $350 a troy ounce).

A small fraction of United States gold reserves is located at the Federal Reserve Bank of New York. The rest is held at Fort Knox, Kentucky; West Point, New York; the Denver and Philadelphia Mints; and the San Francisco Assay Office.

Architectural Capitals

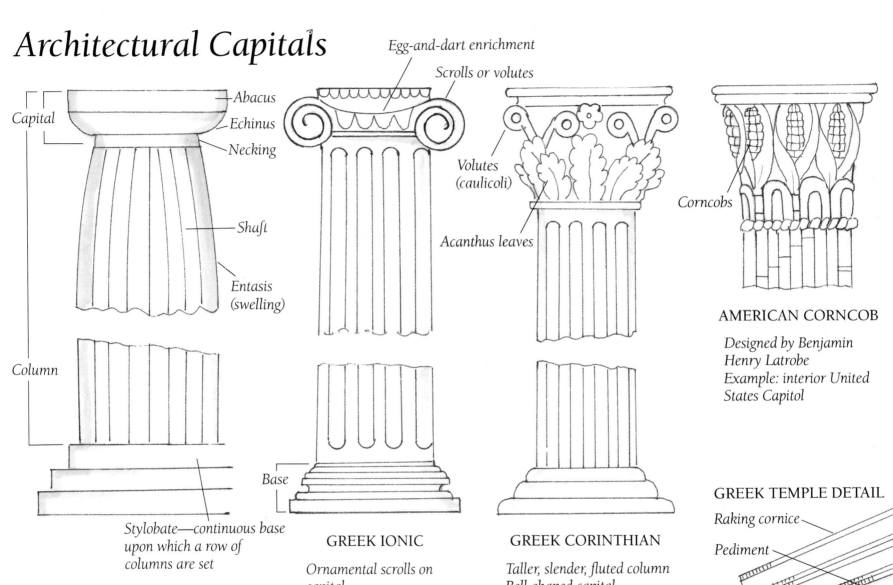

Egg-and-dart enrichment

Scrolls or volutes

Abacus

Echinus

Necking

Capital

Shaft

Entasis
(swelling)

Volutes
(caulicoli)

Acanthus leaves

Corncobs

Column

AMERICAN CORNCOB

*Designed by Benjamin
Henry Latrobe
Example: interior United
States Capitol*

Stylobate—continuous base
upon which a row of
columns are set

GREEK IONIC

*Ornamental scrolls on
capital
Examples: White House,
United States Capitol,
Treasury building*

Base

GREEK CORINTHIAN

*Taller, slender, fluted column
Bell-shaped capital
decorated with caulicoli
and acanthus leaves
Example: United States
Capitol*

GREEK TEMPLE DETAIL

Raking cornice

Pediment

Cornice

Frieze

Entablature

Architrave

GREEK DORIC

*Fluted, heavy shaft does not
rest on a base. Simple
conservative style, feeling of
repose, calm, like trees.
Examples: Lincoln
Memorial, Monticello*

INDEX

Numbers in *italics* refer to illustrations.

architectural capitals, *31*
asterisk (after serial number), 27

Bacon, Henry, 13
Bentsen, Lloyd, 6
Benzing, Joachim C., 10, 13, 21
Berger, Anthony, 12
bills (Federal Reserve notes)
   $1, 3, 7, *7*, 8, 27
   $2, 3, 9, *9*, 10, 11
   $5, 3, 12, *12*, 13, 27
   $10, 14, *14*, *15*
   $20, 16, *16*, 17
   $50, 3, 4, 18, *18*, 19
   $100, 20, 21
   $500, 22, *22*, 27
   $1,000, 23, *23*
   $5,000, 24, *24*
   $10,000, 25
   $100,000, 26
   face of (parts identified), *4*
   size of, 3
   slang for, 3, 28
Brady, Mathew, 12
Brooks, Charles A., 17
Bureau of Engraving and Printing, 5, 26
Burt, Charles, 9, 12

Capitol, United States, 19, *19*, 31
Chase, Salmon P., 3, 4, 25, *25*, 28
check letter/face-plate number, 4, 27, *27*
Cleveland, Grover, 23, *23*
counterfeiting, 4, 6, 28–29, *29*

Declaration of Independence, 11

signing of, *9*, 11, *11*, 21

Eissler, John, 18, 20, 22, 23

Federal Reserve Bank/System, 4, 30, *30*
   number on a bill, 4
   seal, 4
Franklin, Benjamin, 3, 4, 11, *11*, 20, *20*
French, Daniel Chester, 13
"FW," 27

Garfield, James, 3
geometric lathe work/bill border, 4, 29
gold bullion reserves, 6, 30, *30*
Grant, Ulysses S., *4*, 12, 18, *18*
Great Seal of the United States, 8, *8*

Hamilton, Alexander, 3, 4, 6, 9, 14, *14*
Hillegas, Michael, 5, *5*
Hoban, James, 17

"In God We Trust," 25
Independence Hall, 21, *21*
inks, 4, 28, 29

Jackson, Andrew, 6, 12, 15, 16, *16*, 17
Jefferson, Thomas, 9, *9*, 10, *11*, 12, 17

King, Martin Luther, Jr., 13

Landress, M. M., 29
Latrobe, Benjamin Henry, 17, 19, 31
Liberty Bell, 21
Lincoln, Abraham, 12, *12*, 17
Lincoln Memorial, 13, *13*, 31

Lister, Thomas, 21

McKinley, William, 18, 22, *22*
Madison, James, 6, 12, 14, 24, *24*
Mellon, Andrew, 3
microprinting, 4, 29
Mills, Robert, 15
Monticello, 10, *10*, 31

paper, 29
portraits on bills, 4, 29

Revere, Paul, 3

Schofield, Louis S., 15, 19
Sealey, Alfred, 16, 24
Secret Service, 5, 28
Secretary of the Treasury, 6, *6*, 14
security thread, 4, 29
serial number, 4, 27
series identification number, 4
Smillie, George F. C., 7, 14, 26
Stuart, Gilbert Charles, 7, 9, 24
Sully, Thomas, 16

Treasurer of the United States, 5, *5*
Treasury, Department of the, 5, 6, 15, *15*,
   31
   seal, 4, 29, 32, *32*
Trumbull, John, 11, 14

Washington, George, 7, *7*, 12, 14, 19
White House, 17, *17*, *24*, 31
Wilson, Woodrow, 26, *26*